Thai

a taste of the East

Thai

a taste of the East

Judy Williams

BARNES & NOBLE

NEW YORK

Cover and internal design by Talking Design.
Recipes by Judy Williams.
Additional text by Linda Doeser.

2006 Barnes & Noble Publishing

ISBN-13: 978-0-7607-8484-6
ISBN-10: 0-7607-8484-1

Printed and bound in China

1 3 5 7 9 10 8 6 4 2

Notes for the Reader
This books uses imperial, metric, and US cup measurements. Follow the same units of
measurement throughout; do not mix imperial and metric. All spoon measurements are
level, unless otherwise stated: teaspoons are assumed to be 5 ml, and tablespoons are
assumed to be 15 ml. Unless otherwise stated, milk is assumed to be whole, eggs and
individual fruits such as bananas are medium, and pepper is freshly ground black
pepper.

Recipes using raw or very lightly cooked eggs should be avoided by infants, the elderly,
pregnant women, convalescents, and anyone suffering from an illness. Pregnant and
breast-feeding women are advised to avoid eating peanuts and peanut products.

contents

introduction

Thais regard eating as one of life's pleasures and great care goes into the preparation and presentation of even the simplest meal. Food must please the eye as well as the taste buds. They love to share meals and the more people gathered around the table, the better. To have to eat alone is thought of as a wretched misfortune.

The balance and harmony of flavor, color, and texture are the keynotes of Thai cuisine and a meal will always offer a combination of hot, sour, sweet, and salty. Dinner is the main meal of the day and includes a number of dishes that are placed on the table at the same time. As well as rice, these might include a fried dish, a steamed dish, a curry, a salad, and a bowl of soup. Ingredients, too, are varied so there will probably be both fish and meat, as well as vegetables. Everyone helps themselves and the dishes are not eaten in any fixed order. Desserts play a more central role in Thailand than in most other Asian countries and include fresh fruits—of which there is an abundance—fritters, and flavored custards.

The other great joy of Thai cooking is the variety and ubiquity of snacks. In every town and city streets are lined with stalls offering all kinds of fried, broiled, and poached dishes and, most frequently of all, noodles. Bicycles and motorcycles are transformed into mobile kitchens, and trucks and carts offer fresh fruit packed on a bed of ice. The aromas are irresistible.

It is no surprise therefore that Thai food has become so popular in the West. Thailand itself is a favorite destination for vacations and is also much visited by business travelers. As well as beautiful beaches, fascinating ruins, and magnificent temples, Thai cuisine is an attraction that encourages visitors to return again and again. Now, with the recipes in this book you will be able to enjoy the distinctive flavors and colorful variety of Thai food in your own home.

Historical and regional influences

Thailand lies at a crossroads between India and China and both these countries have had a strong influence on Thai food. The country has seen invasion and conquest yet Thais have never lost their sense of identity or of freedom—indeed, Thailand means land of the free. Rather, they have adopted and adapted foreign imports, making them uniquely their own.

Geographical and cultural diversity have also influenced the development of this complex cuisine. The central plains are perfectly suited to growing rice, a staple throughout the country and an important export. Vegetables and a huge variety of tropical fruits are grown here, many of which find their way to the thronging markets of Bangkok which is also located in this area.

The northeast of the country is a high, drier plateau, eventually sloping up into the mountains. This is an area susceptible to drought and is the most infertile part of the country, although rice has been grown here for millennia. Chiles are also produced in abundance.

The northern city of Chiang Mai, famous for its cuisine, especially its signature dish of noodle soup, is located close to the country's borders with both Myanmar, formerly Burma, and Laos, both of which have strongly influenced its style of cooking. In this region, pork is more prevalent than chicken or beef, just as it is in Burmese curries. Coconut palms do not grow here so the flavor and thickness of coconut milk are not characteristics of northern curries as they are in the south.

The long east coastline and the shorter west coastline of the peninsula provide a rich source of all kinds of seafood, while inland there are palm plantations and fruit is grown. Coconut milk is widely used in southern dishes and so too is palm sugar.

The Thai kitchen

Most of the equipment needed to prepare the recipes in this book will be found in any well-stocked western kitchen—a set of cook's knives, cutting boards (separate ones for meat, fish, and vegetables), measuring cups, slotted spoons, etc.

A wok is essential and is often the only pan required. It is worth buying a heavy carbon steel or cast iron wok with deep sides and a diameter of around 14 inches. Woks are available with a single long handle or two ear-shaped handles and some are supplied with a lid. Lids can also be bought separately. Before using a new wok, you will probably need to scrub off the manufacturer's protective coating of oil and season it according to the manufacturer's instructions. Once seasoned, it should be washed only in hot water without detergent. Nonstick woks do not require seasoning.

A steamer with a flat base is also essential if you want to cook little packets of food or glutinous rice balls. Stacking bamboo steamers, available from Chinese supermarkets and specialty stores, are ideal and inexpensive.

While not essential, you might like to consider buying an electric rice cooker. This is a fail-safe way of cooking rice and easier to wash than a conventional pan.

Thais rarely follow recipes, having learned the art of cooking from observing and helping previous generations and in Thailand cooking really is an art. Looking, smelling, tasting, and feeling the texture are essential for achieving just the right balance of flavors, the required degree of heat, and the desired thickness of a sauce. While the recipes in this book specify quantities, you are advised to adopt this Thai method of cooking and adjust dishes to suit your family's taste.

Curry paste

There's nothing wrong with using prepared curry pastes—the authentic ones save time and effort and are usually of excellent quality. However, it is more fun to have a go yourself. Homemade curry pastes take time to make but the flavors will be fresher and stronger than those of the bottled versions. Always use good-quality, fresh ingredients, as the final product will last longer and taste better. The following curry pastes may be stored in the refrigerator for up to 3 weeks and used as required. Alternatively, they may be frozen and thawed before use. Although the quantities of the ingredients differ in green and red curry paste, the method for making them is the same.

Green curry paste

1 tbsp. coriander seeds
1 tbsp. cumin seeds
1 tsp. shrimp paste
15 green Thai chiles, chopped
2 shallots, chopped
6 garlic cloves, chopped
1-inch piece of galangal, chopped
2 lemongrass stalks, chopped
6 kaffir lime leaves
2 tbsp. chopped cilantro root
grated rind of 1 lime
1 tsp. salt
1 tsp. black peppercorns

Red curry paste

1 tbsp. coriander seeds
1 tbsp. cumin seeds
2 tsp. shrimp paste
12 red Thai or bird chiles, chopped
2 shallots, chopped
8 garlic cloves, chopped
1-inch piece of galangal, chopped
2 lemongrass stalks, chopped
4 kaffir lime leaves, chopped
2 tbsp. chopped cilantro root
grated rind of 1 lime
1 tsp. black peppercorns

1 Dry-fry the coriander and cumin seeds in a heavy skillet, stirring constantly, for 2–3 minutes, until they give off their aroma. Remove from the heat and grind to a powder with a mortar and pestle, spice grinder, or blender.

2 Wrap the shrimp paste in a piece of foil and broil or dry-fry, turning once, for 2–3 minutes.

3 Put the ground spices, unwrapped shrimp paste, and chiles in a blender or food processor and process until finely chopped. Add the remaining ingredients and process again to a smooth paste.

Essential ingredients in Thai food

Nowadays many exotic ingredients are available from supermarkets. If you are having difficulty finding a particular Thai ingredient, a Chinese supermarket or specialty store will be the place to look.

BASIL: Three varieties of this pungent herb are used in Thai cooking—lemon basil, sweet basil, and Thai or Holy basil. They are all slightly stronger in flavor than western basil, but this may be used as a substitute.

CHILE: This is a keynote flavor. The most popular type is the very fiery Thai chile, which may be red or green.

COCONUT MILK: Available in cans, this is an unsweetened liquid made by combining grated fresh coconut and water.

CURRY PASTE: This is what gives Thai curries their characteristic flavor. Prepared red, green, and yellow curry pastes are widely available and usually of excellent quality. Make sure that you buy Thai curry paste, not Indian. Homemade pastes are delicious but a little time-consuming.

FISH SAUCE: Also known as nam pla, this is made from salted anchovies. Thais use this flavoring in the same way and as often as the Chinese use soy sauce.

GALANGAL: A member of the ginger family, this root looks similar to gingerroot and is prepared in the same way. It has a sharp, lemon-like flavor.

GARLIC: Used in almost all savory Thai recipes, usually added at the beginning.

KAFFIR LIME LEAVES: Dried leaves are widely available and Chinese supermarkets often stock fresh ones, which keep well and can be frozen. Thais use them like westerners use bay leaves.

LEMONGRASS: Looking like a scallion, lemongrass is very aromatic. Only the bulb and bottom 3–4 inches are used as the stalks are woody. It must be very finely chopped or, alternatively, removed from the dish before serving.

MAGIC PASTE: To make your own magic paste, peel the cloves from 1 whole bulb of garlic and, using a mortar and pestle, grind with a bunch of fresh cilantro leaves and roots and ½ cup white peppercorns.

NOODLES: Rice noodles, rice vermicelli, egg noodles, and cellophane noodles (also known as glass, transparent, and bean thread noodles) are all used in Thai cooking.

PALM SUGAR (JAGGERY): This hard, brown sugar made from coconut palm sap may be difficult to find. If so, substitute brown sugar.

RICE: There are two main types used in Thailand. Glutinous or sticky rice has a short grain and can be rolled into balls. It is used for both savory and sweet dishes. Jasmine or fragrant rice has a long grain and may be boiled or steamed, usually without the addition of salt.

SHRIMP PASTE: A thick paste with a very strong smell made from dried salted shrimp. Use in small amounts as its flavor is very intense.

chapter 1
light bites

hot-&-sour soup

tom yam

SERVES 4

6 dried shiitake mushrooms

4 oz. rice vermicelli noodles

4 small fresh green chiles, seeded and chopped

6 tbsp. rice vinegar

3½ cups vegetable stock

2 lemongrass stalks, snapped in half

4 oz. canned water chestnuts, drained, rinsed,
  and halved

6 tbsp. Thai soy sauce

juice of 1 lime

1 tbsp. jaggery or brown sugar

3 scallions, chopped, to garnish

1. Place the dried mushrooms in a bowl and pour in enough hot water to cover. Set aside to soak for 1 hour. Place the noodles in another bowl and pour in enough hot water to cover. Set aside to soak for 10 minutes. Combine the chiles and rice vinegar in a third bowl and set aside.

2. Drain the mushrooms and noodles. Bring the stock to a boil in a large pan. Add the mushrooms, noodles, lemongrass, water chestnuts, soy sauce, lime juice, and sugar, and bring to a boil.

3. Stir in the chile and vinegar mixture and cook for 1–2 minutes. Remove and discard the lemongrass. Ladle the soup into warmed bowls and serve hot, garnished with the scallions.

shrimp laksa
khung

SERVES 4

14 oz. canned coconut milk

1¼ cups vegetable stock

1¾ oz. vermicelli rice noodles

1 red bell pepper, seeded and cut into strips

8 oz. canned bamboo shoots, drained and rinsed

2-inch piece fresh ginger, sliced thinly

3 scallions, chopped

1 tbsp. Thai red curry paste

2 tbsp. fish sauce

1 tsp. jaggery or brown sugar

6 sprigs fresh Thai basil

12 unshelled cooked shrimp

1. Pour the coconut milk and stock into a pan and bring slowly to a boil. Add the remaining ingredients, except the shrimp, and let simmer gently for 4–5 minutes, until the noodles are cooked.

2. Add the shrimp and let simmer for an additional 1–2 minutes, until heated through. Ladle the soup into small, warmed bowls, dividing the shrimp equally among them, and serve.

corn & crab soup
tom jood pu sai khow pod

SERVES 4

2 tbsp. vegetable or peanut oil

4 garlic cloves, chopped finely

5 shallots, chopped finely

2 lemongrass stalks, chopped finely

1-inch piece fresh ginger, chopped finely

4 cups chicken stock

14 oz. canned coconut milk

scant 1½ cups frozen corn kernels

12 oz. canned crabmeat, drained and shredded

2 tbsp. fish sauce

juice of 1 lime

1 tsp. jaggery or brown sugar

bunch of fresh cilantro, chopped, to garnish

1. Heat the oil in a large skillet and sauté the garlic, shallots, lemongrass, and ginger over low heat, stirring occasionally, for 2–3 minutes, until softened. Add the stock and coconut milk and bring to a boil. Add the corn, reduce the heat, and let simmer gently for 3–4 minutes.

2. Add the crabmeat, fish sauce, lime juice, and sugar, and let simmer gently for 1 minute. Ladle into warmed bowls, garnish with the chopped cilantro, and serve immediately.

spicy beef & noodle soup

guay tiaw tom yam nuea

SERVES 4

4 cups beef stock

⅔ cup vegetable or peanut oil

3 oz. rice vermicelli noodles

2 shallots, sliced thinly

2 garlic cloves, crushed

1-inch piece fresh ginger, sliced thinly

8-oz. piece beef tenderloin, cut into thin strips

2 tbsp. Thai green curry paste

2 tbsp. Thai soy sauce

1 tbsp. fish sauce

chopped fresh cilantro, to garnish

1. Pour the stock into a large pan and bring to a boil. Meanwhile, heat the oil in a wok or large skillet. Add a third of the noodles and cook for 10–20 seconds, until they have puffed up. Lift out with tongs, drain on paper towels, and set aside. Discard all but 2 tablespoons of the oil.

2. Add the shallots, garlic, and ginger to the wok or skillet and stir-fry for 1 minute. Add the beef and curry paste and stir-fry for an additional 3–4 minutes, until tender.

3. Add the beef mixture, the uncooked noodles, soy sauce, and fish sauce to the pan of stock and let simmer for 2–3 minutes, until the noodles have swelled. Serve hot, garnished with the chopped cilantro and the reserved crispy noodles.

crispy egg rolls
po pia thot

SERVES 4

2 tbsp. vegetable or peanut oil

6 scallions, cut into 2-inch lengths

1 fresh green chile, seeded and chopped

1 carrot, cut into thin sticks

1 zucchini, cut into thin sticks

½ red bell pepper, seeded and thinly sliced

¾ cup bean sprouts

4 oz. canned bamboo shoots, drained and rinsed

3 tbsp. Thai soy sauce

1–2 tbsp. chili sauce

8 egg roll wrappers

vegetable or peanut oil, for deep-frying

1. Heat the oil in a wok and stir-fry the scallions and chile for 30 seconds. Add the carrot, zucchini, and red bell pepper and stir-fry for 1 minute more. Remove the wok from the heat and stir in the bean sprouts, bamboo shoots, soy sauce, and chili sauce. Taste and add more soy sauce or chili sauce if necessary.

2. Place an egg roll wrapper on a counter and spoon some of the vegetable mixture diagonally across the center. Roll one corner over the filling and flip the sides of the wrapper over the top to enclose the filling. Continue to roll up to make an enclosed package. Repeat with the remaining wrappers and filling to make 8 egg rolls.

3. Heat the oil for deep-frying in a wok or large skillet. Deep-fry the egg rolls, 3–4 at a time, until crisp and golden brown. Remove with a slotted spoon, drain on paper towels while you cook the remainder, then serve immediately.

wontons
kaeow

SERVES 4

for the filling

2 tbsp. vegetable or peanut oil

6 scallions, chopped

4½ oz. white mushrooms, chopped

2 oz. haricots verts, chopped

2 oz. corn kernels, drained if canned

1 egg, beaten

3 tbsp. Thai soy sauce

1 tbsp. jaggery or brown sugar

½ tsp. salt

for the wontons

24 wonton wrappers

1 egg, beaten

vegetable or peanut oil, for deep-frying

plum or chili sauce, to serve

1. To make the filling, heat the oil in a preheated wok and stir-fry the scallions, mushrooms, and haricots verts for 1–2 minutes, until softened. Add the corn, stir well to mix, and then push the vegetables to the side. Pour in the egg. Stir until lightly set before incorporating the vegetables and adding the soy sauce, sugar, and salt. Remove the wok from the heat.

2. Place the wonton wrappers in a pile on a counter. Put a teaspoonful of the filling in the center of the top wrapper. Brush the edges with beaten egg and fold in half diagonally to make a small triangular package. Repeat with the remaining wrappers and filling.

3. Heat the oil for deep-frying in a wok or large skillet. Add the packages, in batches, and deep-fry for 3–4 minutes, until golden brown. Remove from the wok with a slotted spoon and drain on paper towels. Keep warm while you cook the remaining wontons. Serve hot with plum or chili sauce.

vegetable packages
puk hao

SERVES 4

2 tbsp. vegetable or peanut oil

8 oz. potatoes, diced and boiled for 5 minutes

2 garlic cloves, crushed

1 onion, chopped

2 tbsp. Thai green curry paste

scant ½ cup frozen peas, thawed

juice of 1 lime

½ tsp. salt

16 x 4-inch square egg roll wrappers

1 egg, beaten

vegetable or peanut oil, for deep-frying

sweet chili sauce or Thai soy sauce, to serve

1. Heat the oil in a wok or skillet and stir-fry the potatoes, garlic, onion, and curry paste until lightly browned. Stir in the peas, lime juice, and salt, and stir-fry for 1–2 minutes. Remove from the heat.

2. Brush the edges of 1 egg roll wrapper with the beaten egg. Put a small spoonful of the potato mixture in the center and fold up the edges to enclose the filling and make a purse-shaped package. Press the wrapper tightly together to seal the package. Repeat with the remaining wrappers and filling to make 16 small packages.

3. Heat the oil for deep-frying in a wok. Add the vegetable packages, in batches, and deep-fry for 3–4 minutes, until golden brown. Drain on paper towels and keep warm while you cook the remaining packages. Serve hot with a bowl of chili sauce or soy sauce for dipping.

corn fritters
khao ped chup pang

SERVES 4

for the fritters

3 scallions, chopped finely

11½ oz. canned corn kernels, drained

1 red bell pepper, seeded and finely chopped

small handful of fresh cilantro, chopped

2 garlic cloves, crushed

2 eggs

2 tsp. superfine sugar

1 tbsp. fish sauce

2 tbsp. rice flour or cornstarch

vegetable or peanut oil, for pan-frying

for the dip

2 red bell peppers, seeded and halved

2 tomatoes, peeled, seeded, and chopped coarsely

1 tbsp. vegetable or peanut oil, for pan-frying

1 onion, chopped

1 tbsp. Thai red curry paste

3–4 sprigs fresh cilantro, chopped

1. Combine all the ingredients for the fritters in a bowl. Heat the oil in a skillet and cook spoonfuls of the mixture, in batches, until golden brown on the underside. Flip over with a spatula to cook the second side. Remove from the skillet, drain on paper towels, and keep warm.

2. To make the dip, put the red bell peppers on a baking sheet and place, skin-side up, under a hot broiler, until blackened. Using tongs, transfer to a plastic bag, tie the top, and let cool slightly.

3. When the bell peppers are cool enough to handle, peel off the skins and chop the flesh. Put into a blender or food processor with the tomatoes and process until smooth.

4. Heat the oil in a heavy-bottom pan and cook the onion and curry paste for 3–4 minutes, until softened. Add the bell pepper and tomato mixture and cook gently until tender and hot. Stir in the chopped cilantro, cook for 1 minute, and serve hot with the fritters.

omelet rolls
kai yud sai

SERVES 4

4 large eggs

2 tbsp. water

1 tbsp. Thai soy sauce

6 scallions, chopped finely

1 fresh red chile, seeded and chopped finely

1 tbsp. vegetable or peanut oil

1 tbsp. Thai green curry paste

bunch of fresh cilantro, chopped

1. Put the eggs, water, and Thai soy sauce in a bowl. Set aside. Mix together the scallions and chopped chile to form a paste.

2. Heat half the oil in an 8-inch skillet and pour in half the egg mixture. Tilt to coat the bottom of the skillet evenly and cook until set. Lift out and set aside. Heat the remaining oil and make a second omelet in the same way.

3. Spread the scallion and chile paste, and curry paste in a thin layer over each omelet and sprinkle the cilantro on top. Roll up tightly. Cut each one in half and then cut each piece on the diagonal in half again. Serve immediately, while still warm.

fish cakes
thot man pla

SERVES 4

1 lb. white fish fillets, skinned and cut into cubes

1 egg white

2 kaffir lime leaves, torn coarsely

1 tbsp. Thai green curry paste

2 oz. green beans, chopped finely

1 fresh red chile, seeded and chopped finely

bunch of fresh cilantro, chopped

vegetable or peanut oil for cooking

1 fresh green chile, seeded and sliced, to serve

for the dipping sauce

generous ½ cup superfine sugar

¼ cup white wine vinegar

1 small carrot, cut into thin sticks

2-inch piece cucumber, peeled, seeded, and cut into
  thin sticks

1. Put the fish into a food processor with the egg white, lime leaves, and curry paste, and process until smooth. Scrape the mixture into a bowl and stir in the green beans, red chile, and cilantro.

2. With dampened hands, shape the mixture into small patties, about 2 inches across. Place them on a large plate in a single layer and let chill for 30 minutes.

3. Meanwhile, make the dipping sauce. Put the sugar in a pan with 1½ tablespoons water and the vinegar and heat gently, stirring until the sugar has dissolved. Add the carrot and cucumber, then remove from the heat and let cool.

4. Heat the oil in a skillet and cook the fish cakes, in batches, until golden brown on both sides. Drain on paper towels and keep warm while you cook the remaining batches. If desired, reheat the dipping sauce. Serve the fish cakes immediately with warm or cold dipping sauce, topped with chile slices.

crisp sesame shrimp
khung ob gha tord khob

SERVES 4

¾ cup self-rising flour

3 tbsp. sesame seeds, toasted or dry-fried

1 tsp. Thai red curry paste

1 tbsp. fish sauce

⅔ cup water

vegetable or peanut oil, for deep-frying

20 large, uncooked shrimp, shelled with tails intact

chili sauce, for dipping

1. Combine the flour and sesame seeds in a bowl. Stir the curry paste, fish sauce, and water together in a pitcher until mixed. Gradually pour the liquid into the flour, stirring constantly, to make a thick batter.

2. Heat the oil for deep-frying in a wok or large skillet. Holding the shrimp by their tails, dip them into the batter, one at a time, then carefully drop into the hot oil. Cook for 2–3 minutes, until crisp and brown. Drain on paper towels and serve immediately with chili sauce.

crispy wrapped shrimp
khung hau tord khob

SERVES 4

16 large, unpeeled cooked shrimp

juice of 1 lime

4 tbsp. chili sauce

16 wonton wrappers

vegetable or peanut oil, for deep-frying

plum sauce, to serve

1. Remove the heads and shell the shrimp, but leave the tails intact. Place them in a nonmetallic bowl, add the lime juice, and toss lightly to coat. Set aside in a cool place for 30 minutes.

2. Spread a little chili sauce over a wonton wrapper. Place a shrimp diagonally across it, leaving the tail protruding. Fold the bottom corner of the wrapper over the shrimp, fold the next corner up over the head, and then roll the shrimp up in the wrapper so that the body is encased, but the tail is exposed. Repeat with the remaining wrappers, chili sauce, and shrimp.

3. Heat the oil in a wok or skillet and deep-fry the shrimp, in batches, until crisp and browned. Serve hot with plum sauce for dipping.

crab packages
pue hao

SERVES 4

12 oz. canned white crabmeat, drained

1 fresh red chile, seeded and chopped

4 scallions, sliced finely

1 tbsp. Thai red curry paste

juice of ½ lime

½ tsp. salt

20 wonton wrappers

oil for cooking

for the dip

generous ¼ cup superfine sugar

2 tbsp. water

2 tbsp. rice vinegar

3 pieces preserved ginger, sliced

1 tbsp. ginger syrup from the jar

1. Put the crabmeat into a bowl and add the chile, scallions, and curry paste. Stir together with the lime juice and salt.

2. Put the wrappers in a pile and put 1 portion of the crabmeat in the center of the top wrapper. Brush the edges with a little water and roll up the edges to make a small cigar-shaped package. Continue to make packages with the wrappers— you need at least 20.

3. Heat the oil in a wok or large skillet and cook the packages, a few at a time, until golden brown. Drain on paper towels.

4. Put all the ingredients for the dip in a small pan and heat gently until the sugar has melted. Serve warm with the crab packages.

chicken satay
satay gai

SERVES 4

2 tbsp. vegetable or peanut oil

1 tbsp. sesame oil

juice of ½ lime

2 skinless, boneless chicken breasts, cut into
  small cubes

for the dip

2 tbsp. vegetable or peanut oil

1 small onion, chopped finely

1 small fresh green chile, seeded and chopped

1 garlic clove, chopped finely

½ cup crunchy peanut butter

6–8 tbsp. water

juice of ½ lime

1. Combine both the oils and the lime juice in a nonmetallic dish. Add the chicken cubes, cover with plastic wrap, and let chill for 1 hour.

2. To make the dip, heat the oil in a skillet and sauté the onion, chile, and garlic over low heat, stirring occasionally, for about 5 minutes, until just softened. Add the peanut butter, water, and lime juice and let simmer gently, stirring constantly, until the peanut butter has softened enough to make a dip—you may need to add extra water to make a thinner consistency.

3. Meanwhile, drain the chicken cubes and thread them onto 8–12 soaked wooden skewers. Put under a hot broiler or on a barbecue, turning frequently, for about 10 minutes, until cooked and browned. Serve hot with the warm dip.

chapter 2

meals with meat

beef stir-fry
pahd nuea

SERVES 4

2 tbsp. vegetable or peanut oil

2 medium red onions, sliced thinly

2 garlic cloves, chopped

1-inch piece ginger, cut into thin sticks

2 x 4-oz. beef fillets, sliced thinly

1 green bell pepper, seeded and sliced

5½ oz. canned bamboo shoots

¾ cup bean sprouts

2 tbsp. magic paste

1 tbsp. Thai red curry paste

handful of fresh cilantro, chopped

a few sprigs Thai basil

boiled rice, to serve

1. Heat the oil in a wok or large skillet and stir-fry the onions, garlic, and ginger for 1 minute. Add the beef strips and stir-fry over high heat until browned all over. Add the vegetables and the two pastes and cook for 2–3 minutes until blended and cooked.

2. Stir in the cilantro and basil and serve immediately with rice.

coconut beef curry

kaeng ped ka-ti nuea

SERVES 4

for the Mussaman Curry Paste

4 large dried red chiles

2 tsp. shrimp paste

3 shallots, chopped finely

3 garlic cloves, chopped finely

1-inch piece fresh galangal, chopped finely

2 lemongrass stalks (white part only), chopped finely

2 whole cloves

1 tbsp. coriander seeds

1 tbsp. cumin seeds

seeds from 3 cardamom pods

1 tsp. black peppercorns

1 tsp. salt

1 tbsp. ground coriander

1 tbsp. ground cumin

3 tbsp. Mussaman Curry Paste

½ cup water

2¾ oz. block creamed coconut

1 lb. beef tenderloin, cut into strips

1¾ cups coconut milk

½ cup unsalted peanuts, chopped finely

2 tbsp. fish sauce

1 tsp. jaggery or brown sugar

4 kaffir lime leaves

boiled rice with chopped fresh cilantro, to serve

1. First make the curry paste. Cut off and discard the chile stalks and place the chiles in a bowl. Cover with hot water and set aside to soak for 30–45 minutes. Wrap the shrimp paste in foil and broil or dry-fry for 2–3 minutes, turning once or twice. Remove from the broiler or skillet. Dry-fry the shallots, garlic, galangal, lemongrass, cloves, coriander, cumin, and cardamom seeds over low heat, stirring frequently, for 3–4 minutes, until lightly browned. Transfer to a food processor and process until finely ground. Add the chiles and their soaking water, peppercorns, and salt, and process again. Add the shrimp paste and process again to a smooth paste, scraping down the sides as necessary.

2. Combine the coriander, cumin, and curry paste in a bowl. Pour the measured water into a pan, add the creamed coconut, and heat until it has dissolved. Add the curry paste mixture and let simmer for 1 minute.

3. Add the beef and let simmer for 6–8 minutes, then add the coconut milk, peanuts, fish sauce, and sugar. Let simmer gently for 15–20 minutes, until the meat is tender.

4. Add the lime leaves and let simmer for 1–2 minutes. Serve the curry hot with rice with freshly chopped cilantro stirred through it.

beef with fresh noodles
guay tiaw nuea

SERVES 4

6 dried black cloud Chinese mushrooms

2 tbsp. vegetable or peanut oil

2 x 8-oz. sirloin steaks, sliced thickly

1 onion, cut into thin wedges

2 garlic cloves, chopped

1 green bell pepper, seeded and chopped

3 celery stalks, sliced

2 tbsp. Thai green curry paste

1¼ cups beef stock

4 tbsp. black bean sauce

8 oz. fresh egg noodles

4 tbsp. chopped fresh parsley

1. Put the mushrooms in a bowl, cover with boiling water, and set aside to soak for 30 minutes. Drain. Break up any larger pieces.

2. Heat the oil in a wok and stir-fry the steak over high heat until browned. Add the mushrooms, onion, garlic, bell pepper, and celery, and stir-fry for 3–4 minutes. Add the curry paste, beef stock, and black bean sauce, and stir-fry for 2–3 minutes.

3. Meanwhile, cook the noodles in boiling water for 3–4 minutes, drain well, and stir into the wok. Sprinkle the parsley over and stir. Serve immediately.

mussaman curry
kaeng mussaman

SERVES 4

1 tbsp. vegetable or peanut oil

1 lb. top round steak, cut into cubes

2 tbsp. Mussaman Curry Paste (see page 47)

2 large onions, cut into wedges

2 large potatoes, cut into chunks

1¾ cups coconut milk

⅔ cup water

2 cardamom pods

2 tbsp. tamarind paste

2 tsp. jaggery or brown sugar

⅔ cup unsalted peanuts, toasted or dry-fried

1 fresh red chile, sliced thinly

boiled rice, to serve

1. Heat the oil in a wok and cook the meat, in batches, until browned all over. Remove with a slotted spoon and set aside.

2. Add the curry paste to the wok and stir-fry for 1–2 minutes. Add the onions and potatoes and stir-fry for 4–5 minutes, until golden brown. Remove with a slotted spoon and set aside.

3. Pour the coconut milk into the wok with the measured water and bring to a boil. Reduce the heat and let simmer for 8–10 minutes.

4. Return the meat and cooked vegetables to the wok. Add the cardamom, tamarind paste, and sugar, and let simmer for 15–20 minutes, until the meat is tender. Stir in the peanuts and chile and serve with rice.

beef with onions & broccoli

pud nuea sai hom-yai la thai broccoli

SERVES 4

2 tbsp. vegetable or peanut oil

2 tbsp. Thai green curry paste

2 x 6-oz. sirloin steaks, sliced thinly

2 onions, sliced

6 scallions, chopped

2 shallots, chopped finely

8 oz. broccoli, cut into florets

1¾ cups coconut milk

3 kaffir lime leaves, chopped coarsely

4 tbsp. chopped fresh cilantro

a few Thai basil leaves

1. Heat the oil in a wok and stir-fry the curry paste for 1–2 minutes. Add the meat, in batches if necessary, and stir-fry until starting to brown.

2. Add the onions, scallions, and shallots, and stir-fry for 2–3 minutes. Add the broccoli and stir-fry for 2–3 minutes.

3. Pour in the coconut milk, add the lime leaves, and bring to a boil. Let simmer gently for 8–10 minutes, until the meat is tender. Stir in the cilantro and basil and serve immediately.

pork with bell peppers
pud moo phrik-thai

SERVES 4

1 tbsp. vegetable or peanut oil

1 tbsp. chili oil

1 lb. pork tenderloin, sliced thinly

2 tbsp. green chili sauce

6 scallions, sliced

1-inch piece fresh ginger, sliced thinly

1 red bell pepper, seeded and sliced

1 yellow bell pepper, seeded and sliced

1 orange bell pepper, seeded and sliced

1 tbsp. fish sauce

2 tbsp. Thai soy sauce

juice of ½ lime

4 tbsp. chopped fresh parsley

cooked flat rice noodles, to serve

1. Heat both the oils in a wok. Add the pork, in batches, and stir-fry until browned all over. Remove with a slotted spoon and set aside.

2. Add the chili sauce, scallions, and ginger to the wok and stir-fry for 1–2 minutes. Add the bell peppers and stir-fry for 2–3 minutes.

2. Return the meat to the wok, stir well, and add the fish sauce, soy sauce, and lime juice. Cook for an additional 1–2 minutes, then stir in the parsley and serve with flat rice noodles.

red curry pork with bell peppers
kaeng moo

SERVES 4

2 tbsp. vegetable or peanut oil

1 onion, coarsely chopped

2 garlic cloves, chopped

1 lb. pork tenderloin, sliced thickly

1 red bell pepper, seeded and cut into squares

6 oz. white mushrooms, quartered

2 tbsp. Thai red curry paste

4 oz. block creamed coconut, chopped

1¼ cups pork or vegetable stock

2 tbsp. Thai soy sauce

4 tomatoes, peeled, seeded, and chopped

handful of fresh cilantro, chopped

boiled noodles or rice, to serve

1. Heat the oil in a wok or large skillet and sauté the onion and garlic for 1–2 minutes, until they are softened but not browned.

2. Add the pork slices and stir-fry for 2–3 minutes until browned all over. Add the bell pepper, mushrooms, and curry paste.

3. Dissolve the coconut in the hot stock and add to the wok with the soy sauce. Bring to a boil and let simmer for 4–5 minutes until the liquid has reduced and thickened.

4. Add the tomatoes and cilantro and cook for 1–2 minutes before serving with noodles or rice.

pork with mixed green beans
pud tua sai mu

SERVES 4

2 tbsp. vegetable or peanut oil

2 shallots, chopped

8 oz. pork tenderloin, sliced thinly

1-inch piece fresh galangal, sliced thinly

2 garlic cloves, chopped

1¼ cups chicken stock

4 tbsp. chili sauce

4 tbsp. crunchy peanut butter

4 oz. haricots verts

generous 1 cup frozen fava beans

4 oz. string beans, sliced

crispy noodles, to serve

1. Heat the oil in a wok and stir-fry the shallots, pork, galangal, and garlic until lightly browned.

2. Add the stock, chili sauce, and peanut butter, and stir until the peanut butter has melted. Add all the beans and let simmer for 3–4 minutes. Serve hot with crispy noodles.

pork & crab meatballs
mu, pu pan kon thot

SERVES 6

8 oz. pork tenderloin, chopped finely

5¾ oz. canned crabmeat, drained

3 scallions, chopped finely

1 garlic clove, chopped finely

1 tsp. Thai red curry paste

1 tbsp. cornstarch

1 egg white

vegetable or peanut oil, for deep-frying

steamed white rice, to serve

for the sauce

1 tbsp. vegetable or peanut oil

2 shallots, chopped

1 garlic clove, crushed

2 large fresh red chiles, seeded and chopped

4 scallions, chopped

3 tomatoes, chopped coarsely

1. Put the pork and crabmeat into a bowl and mix together. Add the scallions, garlic, curry paste, cornstarch, and egg white, and beat well to make a thick paste. With damp hands shape the mixture into walnut-size balls.

2. Heat the oil in a wok and deep-fry the balls, in batches, for 3–4 minutes, turning frequently, until golden brown and cooked. Drain on paper towels and keep warm.

3. To make the sauce, heat the oil in a wok and stir-fry the shallots and garlic for 1–2 minutes. Add the chiles and scallions and stir-fry for 1–2 minutes, then add the tomatoes. Stir together quickly, then spoon the sauce over the pork and crab balls. Serve immediately with rice.

pork with vegetables
pud puk sai moo

SERVES 4

½ cup vegetable or peanut oil

4 oz. rice vermicelli noodles

4 pork belly strips, sliced thickly

1 red onion, sliced

2 garlic cloves, chopped

1-inch piece fresh ginger, sliced thinly

1 large fresh red chile, seeded and chopped

4 oz. baby corn, halved lengthwise

1 red bell pepper, seeded and sliced

6 oz. broccoli, cut into florets

5½ oz. jar black bean sauce

¾ cup bean sprouts

1. Heat the oil in a wok and cook the rice noodles, in batches, for 15–20 seconds, until they puff up. Remove with a slotted spoon, drain on paper towels, and set aside.

2. Pour off all but 2 tablespoons of the oil and stir-fry the pork, onion, garlic, ginger, and chile for 4–5 minutes, or until the meat has browned.

3. Add the corn, red bell pepper, and broccoli and stir-fry for 3–4 minutes, until the vegetables are just tender. Stir in the black bean sauce and bean sprouts, then cook for an additional 2–3 minutes. Serve immediately, topped with the crispy noodles.

pad thai
phat thai

SERVES 4

8 oz. thick rice-stick noodles

2 tbsp. vegetable or peanut oil

2 garlic cloves, chopped

2 fresh red chiles, seeded and chopped

6 oz. pork tenderloin, sliced thinly

4 oz. uncooked shrimp, shelled and chopped

8 fresh Chinese chives or garlic chives, chopped

2 tbsp. fish sauce

juice of 1 lime

2 tsp. jaggery or brown sugar

2 eggs, beaten

¾ cup bean sprouts

4 tbsp. chopped fresh cilantro

¾ cup unsalted peanuts, chopped, plus extra
   to serve

crispy fried onions, to serve

1. Soak the noodles in warm water for 10 minutes, drain well, and set aside.

2. Heat the oil in a wok and stir-fry the garlic, chiles, and pork for 2–3 minutes. Add the shrimp and stir-fry for an additional 2–3 minutes.

3. Add the chives and noodles, then cover and cook for 1–2 minutes. Add the fish sauce, lime juice, sugar, and eggs. Cook, stirring and tossing constantly to mix in the eggs.

4. Stir in the bean sprouts, cilantro, and peanuts, and serve with small dishes of crispy fried onions and extra chopped peanuts.

chapter 3
chicken
& poultry
dishes

green chicken curry
kaeng khiao wan gai

SERVES 4

1 tbsp. vegetable or peanut oil

1 onion, sliced

1 garlic clove, chopped finely

2–3 tbsp. Thai green curry paste

1¾ cups coconut milk

½ cup chicken stock

4 kaffir lime leaves

4 skinless, boneless chicken breasts, cut into cubes

1 tbsp. fish sauce

2 tbsp. Thai soy sauce

grated rind and juice of ½ lime

1 tsp. jaggery or brown sugar

4 tbsp. chopped fresh cilantro, to garnish

1. Heat the oil in a wok or large skillet and stir-fry the onion and garlic for 1–2 minutes, until starting to soften. Add the curry paste and stir-fry for 1–2 minutes.

2. Add the coconut milk, stock, and lime leaves, bring to a boil and add the chicken. Reduce the heat and let simmer gently for 15–20 minutes, until the chicken is tender.

3. Add the fish sauce, soy sauce, lime rind and juice, and sugar. Cook for 2–3 minutes, until the sugar has dissolved. Serve immediately, garnished with chopped cilantro.

chicken with yellow curry sauce

gai pud phung ka-ri

SERVES 4

for the spice paste

6 tbsp. Yellow Curry Paste (see page 134)

⅔ cup plain yogurt

1¾ cups water

handful of fresh cilantro, chopped

handful of fresh Thai basil leaves, shredded

for the stir-fry

2 tbsp. vegetable or peanut oil

2 onions, cut into thin wedges

2 garlic cloves, chopped finely

2 skinless, boneless chicken breasts, cut
    into strips

6 oz. baby corn, halved lengthwise

for the garnish

chopped fresh cilantro

shredded fresh basil

1. To make the spice paste, stir-fry the yellow curry paste in a wok for 2–3 minutes, then stir in the yogurt, water, and herbs. Bring to a boil, then let simmer for 2–3 minutes.

2. Meanwhile, heat the oil in a wok and stir-fry the onions and garlic for 2–3 minutes. Add the chicken and corn and stir-fry for 3–4 minutes, until the meat and corn are tender.

3. Stir in the spice paste and bring to a boil. Let simmer for 2–3 minutes, until heated through. Serve immediately, garnished with extra herbs, if desired.

shredded chicken & mixed mushrooms
gai sai hed ruam

SERVES 4

2 tbsp. vegetable or peanut oil

2 skinless, boneless chicken breasts

1 red onion, sliced

2 garlic cloves, chopped finely

1-inch piece fresh ginger, grated

4 oz. baby white mushrooms

4 oz. shiitake mushrooms, halved

4 oz. cremini mushrooms, sliced

2–3 tbsp. Thai green curry paste

2 tbsp. Thai soy sauce

4 tbsp. chopped fresh parsley

boiled noodles or rice, to serve

1. Heat the oil in a wok and cook the chicken on all sides until lightly browned and cooked through. Remove with a slotted spoon, shred into evenly sized pieces, and set aside.

2. Pour off any excess oil, then stir-fry the onion, garlic, and ginger for 1–2 minutes, until softened. Add the mushrooms and stir-fry for 2–3 minutes, until they start to brown.

3. Add the curry paste, soy sauce, and shredded chicken to the wok and stir-fry for 1–2 minutes. Stir in the parsley and serve immediately with noodles or rice.

ginger chicken with noodles
guay tiaw gai sai khing

SERVES 4

2 tbsp. vegetable or peanut oil

1 onion, sliced

2 garlic cloves, chopped finely

2-inch piece fresh ginger, sliced thinly

2 carrots, sliced thinly

4 skinless, boneless chicken breasts, cut into cubes

1¼ cups chicken stock

4 tbsp. Thai soy sauce

8 oz. canned bamboo shoots, drained and rinsed

2¾ oz. flat rice noodles

for the garnish

4 scallions, chopped

4 tbsp. chopped fresh cilantro

1. Heat the oil in a wok and stir-fry the onion, garlic, ginger, and carrots for 1–2 minutes, until softened. Add the chicken and stir-fry for 3–4 minutes, until the chicken is cooked through and lightly browned.

2. Add the stock, soy sauce, and bamboo shoots, and gradually bring to a boil. Let simmer for 2–3 minutes. Meanwhile, soak the noodles in boiling water for 6–8 minutes. Drain well. Garnish with the scallions and cilantro and serve immediately, with the chicken stir-fry.

egg-fried rice with chicken

khao phat gai sai khai

SERVES 4

generous 1 cup jasmine rice

3 skinless, boneless chicken breasts, cut into cubes

1¾ cups canned coconut milk

1¾ oz. block creamed coconut, chopped

2–3 cilantro roots, chopped

thinly pared rind of 1 lemon

1 fresh green chile, seeded and chopped

3 fresh Thai basil leaves

1 tbsp. fish sauce

1 tbsp. oil

3 eggs, beaten

for the garnish

fresh chives

sprigs fresh cilantro

1. Cook the rice in boiling water for 12–15 minutes, drain well, then let cool and chill overnight.

2. Put the chicken into a pan and cover with the coconut milk. Add the creamed coconut, cilantro roots, lemon rind, and chile, and bring to a boil. Let simmer for 8–10 minutes, until the chicken is tender. Remove from the heat. Stir in the basil and fish sauce.

3. Meanwhile, heat the oil in a wok and stir-fry the rice for 2–3 minutes. Pour in the eggs and stir until they have cooked and mixed with the rice. Line 4 small ovenproof bowls or ramekins with plastic wrap and pack with the rice. Turn out carefully onto serving plates and remove the plastic wrap. Garnish with long chives and sprigs of cilantro. Serve with the chicken.

gingered chicken kabobs
kebab gai khing

SERVES 4

3 skinless, boneless chicken breasts, cut into cubes

juice of 1 lime

1-inch piece fresh ginger, peeled and chopped

1 fresh red chile, seeded and sliced

2 tbsp. vegetable or peanut oil

1 onion, sliced

2 garlic cloves, chopped

1 eggplant, cut into chunks

2 zucchinis, cut into thick slices

1 red bell pepper, seeded and cut into squares

2 tbsp. Thai red curry paste

2 tbsp. Thai soy sauce

1 tsp. jaggery or brown sugar

boiled rice, with chopped cilantro, to serve

1. Put the chicken cubes in a shallow dish. Mix the lime, ginger, and chile together and pour over the chicken pieces. Stir gently to coat. Cover and let chill for at least 3 hours to marinate.

2. Thread the chicken pieces onto soaked wooden skewers and cook under a hot broiler for 3–4 minutes, turning often, until cooked through.

3. Meanwhile, heat the oil in a wok or large skillet and sauté the onion and garlic for 1–2 minutes, until softened but not browned. Add the eggplant, zucchini, and bell pepper and cook for 3–4 minutes, until cooked but still firm. Add the curry paste, soy sauce, and sugar, and cook for 1 minute.

4. Serve hot with boiled rice, stirred through with chopped cilantro.

ground chicken skewers
gai ping

SERVES 4

2 cups ground chicken

1 onion, chopped finely

1 fresh red chile, seeded and chopped

2 tbsp. Thai red curry paste

1 tsp. jaggery or brown sugar

1 tsp. ground coriander

1 tsp. ground cumin

1 egg white

8 lemongrass stalks

boiled rice with chopped scallion, to serve

1. Combine the chicken, onion, chile, curry paste, and sugar in a bowl and stir well to make a thick paste. Stir in the ground coriander, cumin, and egg white, and mix again.

2. Divide the mixture into 8 equal portions and squeeze them around each of the lemongrass stalks. Arrange on a grill pan and cook over high heat, turning frequently, until browned and cooked through. Serve hot with the rice with the scallion stirred through it.

barbecue chicken
gai yang

SERVES 4

4 cups chicken stock

8 chicken thighs

1 tbsp. lime juice

2 garlic cloves, crushed

2 tbsp. Thai soy sauce

1 tbsp. fish sauce

2 tbsp. chili sauce

1. Bring the stock to a boil in a large wok. Add the chicken and let simmer for 8–10 minutes, until cooked. Remove with a slotted spoon and let cool.

2. Put the cold chicken in a shallow dish. Combine the lime juice, garlic, soy sauce, fish sauce, and chili sauce in a bowl and spoon the mixture over the chicken, turning to coat. Cover with plastic wrap and let chill for 2–3 hours.

3. Cook the chicken thighs over hot coals, turning them frequently and brushing with the marinade, for 8–10 minutes, until browned and crisp. Serve hot or cold.

red chicken salad
yum ped daeng

SERVES 4

4 skinless, boneless chicken breasts

2 tbsp. Thai red curry paste

2 tbsp. vegetable or peanut oil

1 head of Napa cabbage, shredded

6 oz. bok choy, torn into large pieces

½ head of savoy cabbage, shredded

2 shallots, chopped finely

2 garlic cloves, crushed

1 tbsp. rice vinegar

2 tbsp. sweet chili sauce

2 tbsp. Thai soy sauce

1. Slash the flesh of the chicken several times and rub the curry paste into each cut. Cover and let chill overnight.

2. Cook the chicken in a heavy-bottom pan over medium heat or on a grill pan for 5–6 minutes, turning once or twice, until cooked through. Keep warm.

3. Heat 1 tablespoon of the oil in a wok or large skillet and stir-fry the Napa cabbage, bok choy, and savoy cabbage until just wilted. Add the remaining oil, shallots, and garlic, and stir-fry until just tender but not browned. Add the vinegar, chili sauce, and soy sauce. Remove from the heat.

4. Arrange the greens on 4 serving plates. Slice the chicken, arrange on the salad greens, and drizzle the hot dressing over. Serve immediately.

duck salad
yum ped

SERVES 4

4 boneless duck breasts, skin on

1 lemongrass stalk, broken into thirds and each
  cut in half lengthwise

3 tbsp. vegetable or peanut oil

2 tbsp. sesame oil

1 tsp. fish sauce

1 fresh green chile, seeded and chopped

2 tbsp. Thai red curry paste

½ fresh pineapple, peeled and sliced

3-inch piece cucumber, peeled, seeded, and sliced

3 tomatoes, cut into wedges

1 onion, sliced thinly

for the dressing

juice of 1 lemon

2 garlic cloves, crushed

1 tsp. jaggery or brown sugar

2 tbsp. vegetable or peanut oil

1. Unwrap the duck and let the skin dry out overnight in the refrigerator.

2. The following day, slash the skin side 5 or 6 times. Mix the lemongrass, 2 tablespoons of the vegetable oil, all the sesame oil, fish sauce, chile, and curry paste together in a shallow dish and place the duck breasts in the mixture. Turn to coat and to rub the marinade into the meat. Let chill for 2–3 hours.

3. Heat the remaining oil in a wok or large skillet and cook the duck, skin-side down, over medium heat for 3–4 minutes until the skin is browned and crisp and the meat cooked most of the way through.

4. Turn the breasts over and cook until browned and the meat is cooked to your liking.

5. Meanwhile, arrange the pineapple, cucumber, tomatoes, and onion on a platter. Mix the dressing ingredients together and pour over the top.

6. Lift the duck out of the wok and slice thickly. Arrange the duck slices on top of the salad and serve while still hot.

duck with mixed bell peppers
ped kub phrik thai

SERVES 4

1 tbsp. vegetable or peanut oil

2 duck breasts, skin on

1 onion, sliced

2 garlic cloves, chopped

1 red bell pepper, seeded and chopped

1 green bell pepper, seeded and chopped

1 yellow bell pepper, seeded and chopped

4 tomatoes, peeled, seeded, and chopped

⅔ cup stock

3 tbsp. Thai soy sauce

boiled noodles, to serve

1. Heat the oil in a wok and cook the duck breasts over high heat until crisp and brown. Turn over and cook until cooked through. Lift out and keep warm.

2. Pour off any excess fat and stir-fry the onion and garlic for 2–3 minutes, until softened and lightly browned.

3. Add the bell peppers and stir-fry for 2–3 minutes, until tender. Add the tomatoes, stock, and soy sauce, and let simmer for 1–2 minutes. Transfer to a serving plate. Slice the duck thickly and arrange on top, spooning any sauce over it. Serve with noodles.

chapter 4
fresh from the sea

fish in coconut milk
kaeng ka-ti pla

SERVES 4

2 tbsp. vegetable or peanut oil

6 scallions, chopped coarsely

1-inch piece fresh ginger, grated

2–3 tbsp. Thai red curry paste

1¾ cups coconut milk

⅔ cup fish stock

4 kaffir lime leaves

1 lemongrass stalk, broken in half

12 oz. white fish fillets, skinned and cut into chunks

8 oz. squid rings and tentacles

8 oz. large cooked shelled shrimp

1 tbsp. fish sauce

2 tbsp. Thai soy sauce

4 tbsp. chopped fresh Chinese chives or garlic chives

boiled jasmine rice with chopped fresh cilantro, to serve

1. Heat the oil in a wok or large skillet and stir-fry the scallions and ginger for 1–2 minutes. Add the curry paste and stir-fry for 1–2 minutes.

2. Add the coconut milk, fish stock, lime leaves, and lemongrass. Bring to a boil, then reduce the heat and let simmer for 1 minute.

3. Add the fish, squid, and shrimp, and let simmer for 2–3 minutes, until the fish is cooked. Add the fish and soy sauces and stir in the chives. Serve immediately with jasmine rice with fresh cilantro stirred through it.

fish curry with rice noodles
guay tiaw kaeng pla

SERVES 4

2 tbsp. vegetable or peanut oil

1 large onion, chopped

2 garlic cloves, chopped

3 oz. white mushrooms

8 oz. angler fish, cut into cubes, each about 1 inch

8 oz. salmon fillets, cut into cubes, each about 1 inch

8 oz. cod, cut into cubes, each about 1 inch

2 tbsp. Thai red curry paste

1¾ cups canned coconut milk

handful of fresh cilantro, chopped

1 tsp. jaggery or brown sugar

1 tsp. fish sauce

4 oz. rice noodles

3 scallions, chopped

½ cup bean sprouts

a few Thai basil leaves

1. Heat the oil in a wok or large skillet and gently sauté the onion, garlic, and mushrooms until softened but not browned.

2. Add the fish, curry paste, and coconut milk and bring gently to a boil. Let simmer for 2–3 minutes before adding half of the cilantro, and all of the sugar and fish sauce. Keep warm.

3. Meanwhile, soak the noodles for 3–4 minutes (check the package instructions) or until tender, and drain well through a colander. Put the colander and noodles over a pan of simmering water. Add the scallions, bean sprouts, and most of the basil and steam for 1–2 minutes or until just wilted.

4. Pile the noodles onto warmed serving plates and top with the fish curry. Sprinkle the remaining cilantro and basil over the top and serve immediately.

mixed seafood curry
pok tak

SERVES 4

1 tbsp. vegetable or peanut oil

3 shallots, chopped finely

1-inch piece fresh galangal, peeled and sliced thinly

2 garlic cloves, chopped finely

1¾ cups canned coconut milk

2 lemongrass stalks, snapped in half

4 tbsp. fish sauce

2 tbsp. chili sauce

8 oz. uncooked jumbo shrimp, shelled

8 oz. baby squid, cleaned and sliced thickly

8 oz. salmon fillet, skinned and cut into chunks

6 oz. tuna steak, cut into chunks

8 oz. fresh mussels, scrubbed and debearded

fresh Chinese chives or garlic chives, to garnish

boiled rice, to serve

1. Heat the oil in a large wok and stir-fry the shallots, galangal, and garlic for 1–2 minutes, until they start to soften. Add the coconut milk, lemongrass, fish sauce, and chili sauce. Bring to a boil, reduce the heat, and let simmer for 1–2 minutes.

2. Add the shrimp, squid, salmon, and tuna, and let simmer for 3–4 minutes, until the shrimp have turned pink and the fish is cooked.

3. Check through the mussels and discard any that are open and do not shut when tapped sharply. Add the mussels to the wok and cover with a lid. Let simmer for 1–2 minutes, until they have opened. Discard any mussels that remain closed. Garnish with Chinese chives and serve immediately with rice.

rice with seafood & squid

khao sai khung la pha-muk

SERVES 4

2 tbsp. vegetable or peanut oil

3 shallots, chopped finely

2 garlic cloves, chopped finely

generous 1 cup jasmine rice

1¼ cups fish stock

4 scallions, chopped

2 tbsp. Thai red curry paste

8 oz. baby squid, cleaned and sliced thickly

8 oz. white fish fillets, skinned and cut into cubes

8 oz. salmon fillets, skinned and cut into cubes

4 tbsp. chopped fresh cilantro

1. Heat 1 tablespoon of the oil in a wok and stir-fry the shallots and garlic for 2–3 minutes, until softened. Add the rice and stir-fry for 2–3 minutes.

2. Add a ladleful of the stock and let simmer, adding more stock as needed, for 12–15 minutes, until tender. Transfer to a dish, let cool, and chill overnight.

3. Heat the remaining oil in a wok and stir-fry the scallions and curry paste for 2–3 minutes. Add the squid and fish and stir-fry gently to avoid breaking up the fish. Stir in the rice and cilantro, heat through gently, and serve.

squid & red bell peppers

pud pla-muk sai phrik-deang

SERVES 4

for the spice paste

2 tbsp. vegetable or peanut oil

1 tbsp. chili oil with shrimp

2 shallots, chopped

2–3 large fresh red chiles, seeded and
   chopped coarsely

2 tbsp. ground coriander

2 tbsp. ground cumin

1-inch piece fresh ginger, chopped

1 tbsp. finely chopped lemongrass

3–4 cilantro roots, chopped

1 tsp. salt

1 tsp. jaggery or brown sugar

for the stir-fry

2 red bell peppers, seeded and diced

⅔ cup plain yogurt

1 lb. 10 oz. squid, cleaned and sliced

juice of 1 lime

4 oz. block creamed coconut, chopped

⅔ cup hot water

1. Put all the ingredients for the spice paste into a food processor and process until chopped finely.

2. Scrape the spice paste into a wok and stir-fry gently for 3–4 minutes. Add the red bell peppers and stir-fry for 1–2 minutes.

3. Add the yogurt and bring to a boil. Add the squid and let simmer for 2–3 minutes, then stir in the lime juice, coconut, and water. Let simmer for an additional 1–2 minutes, until the coconut dissolves. Serve immediately.

stir-fried rice noodles with marinated fish

guay tiaw pla

SERVES 4

1 lb. angler fish or cod, cubed

8 oz. salmon fillets, cubed

4 oz. wide rice noodles

2 tbsp. vegetable or peanut oil

2 shallots, sliced

2 garlic cloves, chopped finely

1 fresh red chile, seeded and chopped

2 tbsp. Thai soy sauce

2 tbsp. chili sauce

chopped fresh cilantro, to serve

for the marinade

2 tbsp. vegetable or peanut oil

2 fresh green chiles, seeded and chopped

grated rind and juice of 1 lime

1 tbsp. fish sauce

1. Place the fish in a shallow bowl. To make the marinade, mix the oil, green chiles, lime juice and rind, and fish sauce together and pour over the fish. Cover and chill for 2 hours.

2. Put the noodles in a bowl and cover with boiling water. Leave for 8–10 minutes (check the package instructions) and drain well.

3. Heat the oil in a wok or large skillet and sauté the shallots, garlic, and red chile until lightly browned. Add the soy sauce and chili sauce. Add the fish and the marinade to the wok and stir-fry gently for 2–3 minutes until cooked through.

4. Add the drained noodles and stir gently. Sprinkle with cilantro and serve immediately.

fish curry
kaeng ped pla

SERVES 4

juice of 1 lime

4 tbsp. fish sauce

2 tbsp. Thai soy sauce

1 fresh red chile, seeded and chopped

12 oz. angler fish fillet, cut into cubes

12 oz. salmon fillets, skinned and cut into cubes

1¾ cups coconut milk

3 kaffir lime leaves

1 tbsp. Thai red curry paste

1 lemongrass stalk (white part only), chopped finely

2 cups jasmine rice, boiled

4 tbsp. chopped fresh cilantro

1. Combine the lime juice, half the fish sauce, and the soy sauce in a shallow, nonmetallic dish. Add the chile and the fish, stir to coat, cover with plastic wrap, and chill for 1–2 hours, or overnight.

2. Bring the coconut milk to a boil in a pan and add the lime leaves, curry paste, the remaining fish sauce, and the lemongrass. Let simmer gently for 10–15 minutes.

3. Add the fish and the marinade and let simmer for 4–5 minutes, until the fish is cooked. Serve hot with boiled rice with chopped cilantro stirred through it.

angler fish with lime & chile sauce
yum pla

SERVES 4

4 x 4-oz. angler fish fillets

¼ cup rice flour or cornstarch

6 tbsp. vegetable or peanut oil

4 garlic cloves, crushed

2 large fresh red chiles, seeded and sliced

2 tsp. jaggery or brown sugar

juice of 2 limes

grated rind of 1 lime

boiled rice, to serve

1. Toss the fish in the flour, shaking off any excess. Heat the oil in a wok and cook the fish on all sides until browned and cooked through, taking care when turning not to break it up.

2. Lift the fish out of the wok and keep warm. Add the garlic and chiles and stir-fry for 1–2 minutes, until they have softened.

3. Add the sugar, the lime juice and rind, and 2–3 tablespoons of water and bring to a boil. Let simmer gently for 1–2 minutes, then spoon the mixture over the fish. Serve immediately with rice.

shrimp with scallions & straw mushrooms
kung sai tun-hom la hed

SERVES 4

2 tbsp. vegetable or peanut oil

1 bunch of scallions, chopped

2 garlic cloves, chopped finely

6 oz. block creamed coconut, chopped coarsely

2 tbsp. Thai red curry paste

scant 2 cups fish stock

2 tbsp. fish sauce

2 tbsp. Thai soy sauce

6 sprigs fresh Thai basil

14 oz. canned straw mushrooms, drained

12 oz. large cooked shelled shrimp

boiled jasmine rice, to serve

1. Heat the oil in a wok and stir-fry the scallions and garlic for 2–3 minutes. Add the creamed coconut, red curry paste, and stock, and heat gently until the coconut has dissolved.

2. Stir in the fish sauce and soy sauce, then add the basil, mushrooms, and shrimp. Gradually bring to a boil and serve immediately with jasmine rice.

shrimp with noodles
guay tiaw kung

SERVES 4

1 lb. uncooked jumbo shrimp

1 tbsp. vegetable or peanut oil

3 shallots, chopped finely

2 garlic cloves, chopped finely

1-inch piece fresh ginger, sliced thinly

1¾ cups canned coconut milk

1 tbsp. Thai green curry paste

3–4 fresh Thai basil leaves

1 tsp. jaggery or brown sugar

8 oz. flat rice noodles

2 tsp. sesame oil

2 tbsp. sesame seeds, toasted

a few sprigs fresh Thai basil, to garnish

1. Remove and discard the heads and shell the shrimp. Cut a slit along the back of each and remove and discard the dark vein.

2. Heat the oil in a wok and stir-fry the shallots, garlic, and ginger for 2–3 minutes. Add the coconut milk and curry paste and let simmer for 2–3 minutes.

3. Add the shrimp, basil leaves, and sugar, and cook until the shrimp turn pink.

4. Meanwhile, cook the noodles in boiling water according to the package instructions, then drain well. Stir in the sesame oil and seeds, garnish with the sprigs of basil, and serve immediately with the shrimp.

curried noodles with shrimp & straw mushrooms
guay tiaw kung sai hed

SERVES 4

1 tbsp. vegetable or peanut oil

3 shallots, chopped

1 fresh red chile, seeded and chopped

1 tbsp. Thai red curry paste

1 lemongrass stalk (white part only), chopped finely

8 oz. cooked shelled shrimp

14 oz. canned straw mushrooms, drained

2 tbsp. fish sauce

2 tbsp. Thai soy sauce

8 oz. fresh egg noodles

fresh cilantro, chopped, to garnish

1. Heat the oil in a wok and stir-fry the shallots and chile for 2–3 minutes. Add the curry paste and lemongrass and stir-fry for 2–3 minutes.

2. Add the shrimp, mushrooms, fish sauce, and soy sauce, and stir well to mix.

3. Meanwhile, cook the noodles in boiling water for 3–4 minutes, drain, and transfer to warmed plates. Top with the shrimp curry, sprinkle the cilantro over, and serve immediately.

shrimp with coconut rice
khao ka-ti khung

SERVES 4

1 cup dried shiitake mushrooms

2 tbsp. vegetable or peanut oil

6 scallions, chopped

scant ½ cup dry unsweetened coconut

1 fresh green chile, seeded and chopped

generous 1 cup jasmine rice

½ cup fish stock

1¾ cups coconut milk

12 oz. cooked shelled shrimp

6 sprigs fresh Thai basil

1. Place the mushrooms in a small bowl, cover with hot water, and set aside to soak for 30 minutes. Drain, then cut off and discard the stalks and slice the caps.

2. Heat 1 tablespoon of the oil in a wok and stir-fry the scallions, coconut, and chile for 2–3 minutes, until lightly browned. Add the mushrooms and stir-fry for 3–4 minutes.

3. Add the rice and stir-fry for 2–3 minutes, then add the stock and bring to a boil. Reduce the heat and add the coconut milk. Let simmer for 10–15 minutes, until the rice is tender. Stir in the shrimp and basil, heat through, and serve.

shrimp & papaya salad
somtam gung

SERVES 4

1 papaya, peeled

12 oz. large cooked shrimp, shelled

assorted baby salad greens

for the dressing

4 scallions, chopped finely

2 fresh red chiles, seeded and chopped finely

1 tsp. fish sauce

1 tbsp. vegetable or peanut oil

juice of 1 lime

1 tsp. jaggery or brown sugar

1. Scoop the seeds out of the papaya and discard. Slice the papaya flesh thinly. Stir gently together with the shrimp.

2. Mix the scallions, chiles, fish sauce, oil, lime juice, and sugar together.

3. Arrange the salad greens in a bowl and top with the papaya and shrimp. Pour the dressing over and serve immediately.

crab & cilantro salad
yum pue

SERVES 4

12 oz. canned white crabmeat, drained

4 scallions, finely chopped

handful of fresh cilantro, chopped

1 head of iceberg lettuce, shredded

3-inch piece cucumber, chopped

for the dressing

1 garlic clove, crushed

1-inch piece fresh ginger, peeled and grated

2 lime leaves, torn into pieces

juice of 1 lime

1 tsp. fish sauce

1. Put the crabmeat into a bowl and stir in the scallions and cilantro.

2. Mix the ingredients for the dressing together.

3. Place the lettuce leaves on a serving platter and sprinkle with the cucumber.

4. Arrange the crab salad over the leaves and drizzle the dressing over the salad. Serve immediately.

mixed seafood salad
yum ta-le

SERVES 4

1 lb. fresh mussels, scrubbed and debearded

3 tbsp. vegetable or peanut oil

1 small onion, sliced thinly

8 oz. baby squid, cleaned and sliced

8 oz. cooked shrimp, shelled

1 bunch of scallions, chopped coarsely

1 lemongrass stalk, chopped finely

1 red bell pepper, seeded and cut into strips

½ small head of Napa cabbage, shredded

2 garlic cloves, crushed

1 tsp. fish sauce

1 tsp. jaggery or brown sugar

juice of 1 lemon

2-inch piece cucumber, chopped

1 tomato, seeded and chopped

1. Discard any mussels that are open and do not shut when tapped sharply. Heat 1 tablespoon of the oil in a wok or large skillet and stir-fry the onion, squid, shrimp, and mussels for 1–2 minutes, until the squid is opaque and the mussels have opened. Discard any mussels that remain closed.

2. Mix the scallions, lemongrass, red bell pepper, and Napa cabbage together in a bowl. Add the seafood and stir gently. Transfer to a serving dish.

3. Mix the garlic, the remaining oil, fish sauce, sugar, and lemon juice together. Add the chopped cucumber and tomato, spoon the dressing over the salad and seafood, and serve immediately.

tomato & squid salad
yum pla-muek

SERVES 4

1 lb. tomatoes

1 lb. baby squid, cleaned and left whole

2 garlic cloves, chopped finely

2 fresh green chiles, seeded and sliced

handful of fresh cilantro, chopped

juice of 1 lime

1 tsp. fish sauce

1 tbsp. Thai soy sauce

1. Peel the tomatoes. Cut into quarters, remove all the seeds, and discard them. Finely chop the tomato flesh and set aside.

2. Bring a medium pan of water to a boil, add the squid, and cook for 2–3 minutes. Remove and drain well.

3. Mix the tomatoes, garlic, chiles, and half the cilantro. Add the squid, and toss everything together. Transfer to a serving dish.

4. Mix the lime juice, fish and soy sauces, and the remaining cilantro. Pour the dressing over the salad. Serve warm or cold.

chapter 5
vegetable heaven

eggplant & bean curry
kaeng ped ma khure sai tua

SERVES 4

2 tbsp. vegetable or peanut oil

1 onion, chopped

2 garlic cloves, crushed

2 fresh red chiles, seeded and chopped

1 tbsp. Thai red curry paste

1 large eggplant, cut into chunks

4 oz. baby eggplants, quartered

generous 1 cup baby fava beans

4 oz. haricots verts

1¼ cups vegetable stock

2 oz. block creamed coconut, chopped

3 tbsp. Thai soy sauce

1 tsp. jaggery or brown sugar

3 kaffir lime leaves, torn coarsely

4 tbsp. chopped fresh cilantro

1. Heat the oil in a wok or large skillet and sauté the onion, garlic, and chiles for 1–2 minutes. Stir in the curry paste and cook for 1–2 minutes.

2. Add the eggplants and cook for 3–4 minutes, until starting to soften. (You may need to add a little more oil as eggplants soak it up quickly.) Add all the beans and stir-fry for 2 minutes.

3. Pour in the stock and add the creamed coconut, soy sauce, sugar, and lime leaves. Bring gently to a boil and cook until the coconut has dissolved. Stir in the cilantro and serve hot.

stuffed eggplants
makuea yad sai

SERVES 4

8 small or 4 large eggplants

2 tbsp. vegetable or peanut oil

4 shallots, chopped finely

2 garlic cloves, crushed

2 fresh red chiles, seeded and chopped

1 zucchini, chopped coarsely

4 oz. block creamed coconut, chopped

a few Thai basil leaves, chopped

small handful of fresh cilantro, chopped

4 tbsp. Thai soy sauce

to serve

rice with chopped scallions

sweet chili sauce

1. Preheat the oven to 400°F. Put the eggplants in a roasting pan and cook for 8–10 minutes, until just softened. Cut in half and scoop out the flesh, reserving the shells.

2. Heat the oil in a wok or large skillet and sauté the shallots, garlic, and chiles for 2–3 minutes before adding the zucchini and eggplant flesh. Add the creamed coconut, the herbs, and soy sauce, and let simmer for 3–4 minutes.

3. Divide the mixture among the eggplant shells. Return to the oven for 5–10 minutes, until hot, and serve immediately with rice and sweet chili sauce.

mixed vegetables with quick-fried basil

pud puk ruam ka-preow tord grob

SERVES 4

2 tbsp. vegetable or peanut oil

2 garlic cloves, chopped

1 onion, sliced

4 oz. baby corn, cut in half diagonally

½ cucumber, peeled, halved, seeded, and sliced

8 oz. canned water chestnuts, drained and rinsed

2 oz. snow peas, trimmed

4 oz. shiitake mushrooms

1 red bell pepper, seeded and sliced thinly

1 tbsp. jaggery or brown sugar

2 tbsp. Thai soy sauce

1 tbsp. fish sauce

1 tbsp. rice vinegar

boiled rice, to serve

for the quick-fried basil

vegetable or peanut oil, for cooking

8-12 sprigs fresh Thai basil

1. Heat the oil in a wok and stir-fry the garlic and onion for 1-2 minutes. Add the corn, cucumber, water chestnuts, snow peas, mushrooms, and red bell pepper, and stir-fry for 2–3 minutes, until starting to soften.

2. Add the sugar, soy sauce, fish sauce, and vinegar, and gradually bring to a boil. Let simmer for 1–2 minutes.

3. Meanwhile, heat the oil for the basil in a wok or skillet, and when hot, add the basil sprigs. Cook for 20–30 seconds, until crisp. Remove with a slotted spoon and drain on paper towels.

4. Garnish the vegetable stir-fry with the crispy basil and serve immediately, with the boiled rice.

mixed mushroom stir-fry
pud hed ruem

SERVES 4

2 tbsp. vegetable or peanut oil

6 scallions, sliced

1 tbsp. Thai green curry paste

4 oz. shiitake mushrooms, halved

4 oz. oyster mushrooms

4 oz. white mushrooms

4 oz. portobello mushrooms, sliced

2 tbsp. Thai soy sauce

1 tsp. jaggery or brown sugar

8 oz. canned water chestnuts, drained, rinsed, and sliced

½ cup bean sprouts

cooked noodles, to serve

1. Heat the oil in a wok or skillet and stir-fry the scallions for 30 seconds. Add the curry paste and stir-fry for 1–2 minutes. Add all the mushrooms and stir-fry over high heat until they are tender.

2. Add the soy sauce, sugar, water chestnuts, and bean sprouts and cook for 1–2 minutes, until heated through and just tender. Serve hot with noodles.

carrot & pumpkin curry
kaeng ped carrot kub phuk

SERVES 4

⅔ cup vegetable stock

1-inch piece fresh galangal, sliced

2 garlic cloves, chopped

1 lemongrass stalk (white part only), chopped finely

2 fresh red chiles, seeded and chopped

4 carrots, peeled and cut into chunks

8 oz. pumpkin, peeled, seeded, and cut into cubes

2 tbsp. vegetable or peanut oil

2 shallots, chopped finely

3 tbsp. Yellow Curry Paste

1¾ cups coconut milk

4–6 sprigs fresh Thai basil

⅛ cup toasted pumpkin seeds, to garnish

for the Yellow Curry Paste

3 small fresh orange or yellow chiles, chopped coarsely

3 large garlic cloves, chopped coarsely

4 shallots, chopped coarsely

1 tablespoon ground turmeric

1 tsp. salt

12–15 black peppercorns

1 lemongrass stalk (white part only), chopped coarsely

1-inch piece fresh ginger, chopped

1. Pour the stock into a large pan and bring to a boil. Add the galangal, half the garlic, the lemongrass, and chiles, and let simmer for 5 minutes. Add the carrots and pumpkin and let simmer for 5–6 minutes, until tender.

2. To make the curry paste, put all the ingredients into a food processor or blender and process to a thick paste, scraping down the sides occasionally and making sure the ingredients are well combined.

3. Meanwhile, heat the oil in a wok or skillet and stir-fry the shallots and the remaining garlic for 2–3 minutes. Add the curry paste and stir-fry for 1–2 minutes.

4. Stir the shallot mixture into the pan and add the coconut milk and basil. Let simmer for 2–3 minutes. Serve hot, sprinkled with the toasted pumpkin seeds.

tofu & green vegetable curry
kaeng khiao wan tao hu

SERVES 4

vegetable or peanut oil, for deep-frying

8 oz. firm tofu, drained and cut into cubes

2 tbsp. vegetable or peanut oil

1 tbsp. chili oil

2 fresh green chiles, seeded and sliced

2 garlic cloves, crushed

6 scallions, sliced

2 medium zucchinis, cut into sticks

½ cucumber, peeled, seeded, and sliced

1 green bell pepper, seeded and sliced

1 small head of broccoli, cut into florets

2 oz. haricots verts, halved

scant ½ cup frozen peas, thawed

1¼ cups vegetable stock

2 oz. block creamed coconut, chopped

2 tbsp. Thai soy sauce

1 tsp. jaggery or brown sugar

4 tbsp. chopped fresh parsley, to garnish

1. Heat the oil for deep-frying in a skillet and carefully lower in the tofu cubes, in batches, and cook for 2–3 minutes, until golden brown. Remove with a slotted spoon and drain on paper towels.

2. Heat the other oils in a wok and stir-fry the chiles, garlic, and scallions for 2–3 minutes. Add the zucchinis, cucumber, green bell pepper, broccoli, and haricots verts, and stir-fry for an additional 2–3 minutes.

3. Add the peas, stock, coconut, soy sauce, and sugar. Cover and let simmer for 2–3 minutes, until all the vegetables are tender and the coconut has dissolved.

4. Stir in the tofu and serve immediately, sprinkled with the parsley.

stir-fried rice with green vegetables
khao phat puk

SERVES 4

generous 1 cup jasmine rice

2 tbsp. vegetable or peanut oil

1 tbsp. Thai green curry paste

6 scallions, sliced

2 garlic cloves, crushed

1 zucchini, cut into thin sticks

4 oz. yard-long beans, cut into 3-inch lengths

6 oz. asparagus, trimmed

1 tbsp. fish sauce

3–4 fresh Thai basil leaves

1. Cook the rice in lightly salted boiling water for 12–15 minutes, drain well, then cool thoroughly and chill overnight.

2. Heat the oil in a wok and stir-fry the curry paste for 1 minute. Add the scallions and garlic and stir-fry for 1 minute.

3. Add the zucchini, beans, and asparagus, and stir-fry for 3–4 minutes, until just tender. Break up the rice and add it to the wok. Cook, stirring constantly for 2–3 minutes, until the rice is hot. Stir in the fish sauce and basil leaves. Serve hot.

sweet-&-sour vegetables with cashews

preow wan puk sai tua ob

SERVES 4

1 tbsp. vegetable or peanut oil

1 tsp. chili oil

2 onions, sliced

2 carrots, sliced thinly

2 zucchinis, sliced thinly

small head of broccoli, cut into florets

4 oz. white mushrooms, sliced

4 oz. baby bok choy, halved

2 tbsp. jaggery or brown sugar

2 tbsp. Thai soy sauce

1 tbsp. rice vinegar

scant ½ cup cashews

1. Heat both the oils in a wok or skillet and stir-fry the onions for 1–2 minutes, until they start to soften.

2. Add the carrots, zucchinis, and broccoli, and stir-fry for 2–3 minutes. Add the mushrooms, bok choy, sugar, soy sauce, and rice vinegar, and stir-fry for 1–2 minutes.

3. Meanwhile, dry-fry or toast the cashews. Sprinkle the cashews over the stir-fry and serve immediately.

cauliflower & beans with cashews

daung-ka-lum sai tau khiao, tao ob

SERVES 4

1 tbsp. vegetable or peanut oil

1 tbsp. chili oil

1 onion, chopped

2 garlic cloves, chopped

2 tbsp. Thai red curry paste

1 small cauliflower, cut into florets

6 oz. yard-long beans, cut into 3-inch lengths

⅔ cup vegetable stock

2 tbsp. Thai soy sauce

scant ⅓ cup toasted cashews, to garnish

1. Heat both the oils in a wok and stir-fry the onion and garlic until softened. Add the curry paste and stir-fry for 1–2 minutes.

2. Add the cauliflower and beans and stir-fry for 3–4 minutes, until softened. Pour in the stock and soy sauce and let simmer for 1–2 minutes. Serve immediately, garnished with the cashews.

zucchini & cashew curry
kaeng courgette med mamuang

SERVES 4

2 tbsp. vegetable or peanut oil

6 scallions, chopped

2 garlic cloves, chopped

2 fresh green chiles, seeded and chopped

1 lb. zucchini, cut into thick slices

4 oz. shiitake mushrooms, halved

½ cup bean sprouts

½ cup cashews, toasted or dry-fried

a few Chinese chives or garlic chives, chopped

4 tbsp. Thai soy sauce

1 tsp. fish sauce

rice or noodles, to serve

1. Heat the oil in a wok or large skillet and sauté the scallions, garlic, and chiles for 1–2 minutes, until softened but not browned.

2. Add the zucchinis and mushrooms and cook for 2–3 minutes until tender.

3. Add the bean sprouts, nuts, chives, and both sauces and stir-fry for 1–2 minutes.

4. Serve hot with rice or noodles.

egg-fried rice with vegetables & crispy onions

khao-khai pak horm-tord

SERVES 4

4 tbsp. vegetable or peanut oil

2 garlic cloves, chopped finely

2 fresh red chiles, seeded and chopped

4 oz. white mushrooms, sliced

2 oz. snow peas, halved

2 oz. baby corn, halved

3 tbsp. Thai soy sauce

1 tbsp. jaggery or brown sugar

a few Thai basil leaves

3 cups rice, cooked and cooled

2 eggs, beaten

2 onions, sliced

1. Heat half the oil in a wok or large skillet and sauté the garlic and chiles for 2–3 minutes.

2. Add the mushrooms, snow peas, and corn, and stir-fry for 2–3 minutes before adding the soy sauce, sugar, and basil. Stir in the rice.

3. Push the mixture to one side of the wok and add the eggs to the bottom. Stir until lightly set before combining into the rice mixture.

4. Heat the remaining oil in another skillet and sauté the onions until crispy and brown. Serve the rice topped with the onions.

hot-&-sour vegetable salad

yum puk

SERVES 4

2 tbsp. vegetable or peanut oil

1 tbsp. chili oil

1 onion, sliced

1-inch piece fresh ginger, grated

1 small head of broccoli, cut into florets

2 carrots, cut into short, thin sticks

1 red bell pepper, seeded and cut into squares

1 yellow bell pepper, seeded and cut into strips

2 oz. snow peas, trimmed and halved

2 oz. baby corn, halved

for the dressing

2 tbsp. vegetable or peanut oil

1 tsp. chili oil

1 tbsp. rice vinegar

juice of 1 lime

½ tsp. fish sauce

1. Heat the oils in a wok or large skillet and sauté the onion and ginger for 1–2 minutes until they start to soften. Add the vegetables and stir-fry for 2–3 minutes until they have softened slightly. Remove from the heat and set aside.

2. Mix the dressing ingredients together. Transfer the vegetables to a serving plate and drizzle the dressing over. Serve warm immediately, or let the flavors develop and serve cold.

curried egg salad
yum khai

SERVES 4

6 eggs

1 tbsp. vegetable or peanut oil

1 onion, chopped

1 tbsp. Yellow Curry Paste (see page 134)

4 tbsp. plain yogurt

½ tsp. salt

handful of fresh cilantro, chopped finely

bunch of watercress or arugula

2 zucchinis, cut into short, thin sticks

1 fresh green chile, seeded and chopped finely

1 tsp. fish sauce

1 tsp. rice vinegar

3 tbsp. vegetable or peanut oil

1. Put the eggs in a pan, cover with cold water, and bring to a boil. Let simmer for 10 minutes, then drain and rinse in cold water. Shell and halve.

2. Meanwhile, heat the oil in a medium skillet and sauté the onion gently until softened but not browned. Remove from the heat and stir in the curry paste. Let cool slightly before stirring in the yogurt, salt, and half the cilantro. Set aside.

3. Arrange the watercress and zucchinis on a platter. Mix the chile, fish sauce, vinegar, and oil together and pour the dressing over the leaves.

4. Arrange the eggs on top and spoon the yogurt mixture over each one. Garnish with the remaining cilantro over the top and serve immediately.

eggplant & onion salad
yum makuea

SERVES 4

4 tbsp. vegetable or peanut oil

1 onion, sliced

4 shallots, chopped finely

4 scallions, sliced

12 oz. baby eggplants, quartered

2 tbsp. Thai green curry paste

2 tbsp. Thai soy sauce

1 tsp. jaggery or brown sugar

4 oz. block creamed coconut, chopped

3 tbsp. water

small handful of fresh cilantro, chopped

a few Thai basil leaves, chopped

small handful of fresh parsley, chopped

2½ cups arugula leaves

2 tbsp. sweet chili sauce

1. Heat half the oil in a wok or large skillet and cook the onion, shallots, and scallions together for 1–2 minutes, until just softened but not browned. Lift out and set aside.

2. Cook the eggplant, in batches if necessary, adding more oil as needed, until crisp and golden brown.

3. Return the onions to the wok and add the curry paste, soy sauce, and sugar. Add the creamed coconut and water and cook until dissolved. Stir in most of the cilantro, the basil, and the parsley.

4. Toss the arugula in the chili sauce and serve with the eggplant and onion salad. Garnish with the remaining herbs.

chapter 6
thai-inspired desserts

creamy mango brûlée
mamuang

SERVES 4

2 mangoes

generous 1 cup mascarpone cheese

generous ¾ cup strained plain yogurt

1 tsp. ground ginger

grated rind and juice of 1 lime

2 tbsp. light brown sugar

½ cup raw brown sugar

1. Slice the mangoes on either side of the seed. Discard the seeds and peel the fruit. Slice and then chop the fruit. Divide it between 4 ramekins.

2. Beat the mascarpone cheese with the yogurt. Fold in the ginger, lime rind and juice, and light brown sugar. Divide the mixture among the ramekins and level off the tops. Chill for 2 hours.

3. Sprinkle 2 tablespoons of the raw brown sugar over the top of each dish, covering the creamy mixture. Place under a hot broiler for 2–3 minutes, until melted and browned. Let cool, then chill until needed. This dessert should be eaten on the day it is made.

spicy rice pudding
kau mun

SERVES 4

1¾ cups canned coconut milk

⅔ cup milk

generous ¼ cup light brown sugar

generous ¼ cup short-grain rice

2 tsp. allspice

2 tbsp. butter

1 tsp. ground cinnamon

1. Put the coconut milk and milk in a pan and heat gently. Add the sugar and stir until it has dissolved.

2. Add the rice and allspice and gradually bring to a boil. Let simmer gently, stirring frequently, for 45–60 minutes, until thickened.

3. Stir in the butter, and once it has melted, serve immediately, sprinkled with cinnamon.

mini coconut crêpes
kanum buang ma-prow oon

SERVES 4

2 oz. block creamed coconut, chopped

⅔ cup boiling water

1½ cups all-purpose flour

2 tbsp. superfine sugar

2 eggs

generous 1¾ cups milk

¼ cup shredded unsweetened dried coconut

4 tbsp. butter

½ melon, seeded, peeled, and sliced thinly

1. Put the creamed coconut in a bowl, pour in the measured water, and stir until dissolved.

2. Sift the flour into another bowl and stir in the sugar. Beat in the eggs and half the milk. Gradually beat in the remaining milk and then the coconut mixture to make a creamy batter. Stir in the unsweetened coconut.

3. Melt a little of the butter in a heavy-bottom skillet. Add 3–4 tablespoons of the batter, spacing them well apart as they will spread during cooking. Cook for 1–2 minutes, then flip over to cook the second side. Remove from the skillet and keep warm. Cook the remaining batter in the same way. Serve warm with melon slices.

banana-stuffed crêpes
pang ho khuay

SERVES 4

1½ cups all-purpose flour

2 tbsp. light brown sugar

2 eggs

generous 1¾ cups milk

grated rind and juice of 1 lemon

4 tbsp. butter

3 bananas

4 tbsp. corn syrup

1. Combine the flour and sugar and beat in the eggs and half the milk. Beat together until smooth. Gradually add the remaining milk, stirring constantly to make a smooth batter. Stir in the lemon rind.

2. Melt a little butter in an 8-inch skillet and pour in one-quarter of the batter. Tilt the skillet to coat the bottom and cook for 1–2 minutes, until set. Flip the crêpe over and cook the second side. Slide out of the skillet and keep warm. Repeat to make 3 more crêpes.

3. Slice the bananas and toss in the lemon juice. Pour the syrup over them and toss together. Fold each crêpe in half and then in half again and fill the center with the banana mixture. Serve warm.

grilled bananas
khuay ping

SERVES 4

2 oz. block creamed coconut, chopped

⅔ cup heavy cream

4 bananas

juice and rind of 1 lime

1 tbsp. vegetable or peanut oil

scant ½ cup shredded unsweetened dried coconut

1. Put the creamed coconut and cream in a small pan and heat gently until the coconut has dissolved. Remove from the heat and set aside to cool for 10 minutes, then whisk until thick but floppy.

2. Peel the bananas and toss in the lime juice and rind. Lightly oil a preheated grill pan and cook the bananas, turning once, for 2–3 minutes, until soft and browned.

3. Toast the dried coconut on a piece of foil under a broiler until lightly browned. Serve the bananas with the coconut cream, sprinkled with the toasted coconut.

ginger creams & sesame pastries
ka-num rung ob yha rad na khing

SERVES 4

generous 1¾ cups heavy cream

⅔ cup plain yogurt

4 tbsp. ginger syrup (from the preserved ginger jar)

6 pieces preserved ginger, chopped

4 tbsp. brown sugar

4 x 8-inch sheets filo pastry

4 tbsp. butter, melted

3 tbsp. sesame seeds

1. Whip the cream until thick but not floppy. Stir in the yogurt and the ginger syrup. Divide the preserved ginger among 4 glasses or cups and then top with the ginger cream. Sprinkle 1 tablespoon of sugar on each one and let chill overnight.

2. Preheat the oven to 400°F. Cut the filo pastry into sixteen 4-inch squares. Brush 1 square with melted butter, then place another square on top. Repeat twice more to make a 4-layered pastry. Make 3 more in the same way.

3. Brush with butter and sprinkle with sesame seeds and bake for 10–15 minutes, until golden brown. Serve warm with the ginger creams.

mixed fruit salad
polamai ruam

SERVES 4

1 papaya, halved, peeled, and seeded

2 bananas, sliced thickly

1 small pineapple, peeled, halved, cored, and sliced

12 litchis, peeled if fresh

1 small melon, seeded and cut into thin wedges

2 oranges

grated rind and juice of 1 lime

2 tbsp. superfine sugar

1. Arrange the papaya, bananas, pineapple, litchis, and melon on a serving platter. Cut off the rind and pith from the oranges. Cut the orange slices out from between the membranes and add to the fruit platter. Grate a small quantity of the discarded orange rind and add to the platter.

2. Combine the lime rind, juice, and sugar. Pour over the salad and serve.

roasted spicy pineapple
subparot ob

SERVES 4

1 pineapple

1 mango, peeled, seeded, and sliced

4 tbsp. butter

4 tbsp. corn syrup

1–2 tsp. cinnamon

1 tsp. freshly grated nutmeg

4 tbsp. brown sugar

2 passion fruits

⅔ cup sour cream

finely grated rind of 1 orange

1. Preheat the oven to 400°F. Use a sharp knife to cut off the top, base, and skin of the pineapple, then cut into quarters. Remove the central core and cut the flesh into large cubes. Place them in a roasting pan with the mango.

2. Place the butter, syrup, cinnamon, nutmeg, and sugar in a small pan and heat gently, stirring constantly, until melted. Pour the mixture over the fruit. Roast for 20–30 minutes, until the fruit is browned.

3. Halve the passion fruits and scoop out the seeds. Spoon over the roasted fruit. Mix the sour cream and orange rind together and serve with the fruit.

banana & coconut ice cream
i tim ma-prown sai khuay

SERVES 6–8

3 oz. block creamed coconut, chopped

2½ cups heavy cream

½ cup confectioners' sugar

2 bananas

1 tsp. lemon juice

fresh fruit, to serve

1. Put the creamed coconut in a small bowl. Add just enough boiling water to cover and stir until dissolved. Let cool.

2. Whip the cream with the confectioners' sugar until thick but still floppy. Take care not to overwhip the cream or it will curdle when the other ingredients are added. Mash the bananas with the lemon juice and whisk gently into the cream, along with the cold coconut.

3. Transfer to a freezerproof container and freeze overnight. Serve in scoops with fresh fruit.

pineapple & lime sherbet
subparot, ma-nau i tim

SERVES 4

generous 1 cup superfine sugar

2½ cups water

grated rind and juice of 2 limes

1 small pineapple, peeled, quartered, and chopped

sugar cookies, to serve

1. Put the sugar and water into a pan and heat gently, stirring until the sugar has dissolved. Bring to a boil and let simmer for 10 minutes.

2. Stir in the grated rind and half the lime juice. Remove from the heat and let cool.

3. Put the pineapple in a blender or food processor and process until smooth. Add to the cold syrup with the remaining lime juice. Pour into a freezerproof container and freeze until crystals have formed around the edge.

4. Turn out the sherbet into a bowl. Beat well with a fork to break up the crystals. Return to the freezer and chill overnight. If liked, you can halve two pineapples, cut out the flesh (use the flesh of one in the sherbet and reserve the remainder for another recipe), and use the shells as attractive bowls for serving scoops of the sherbet. Serve with the sugar cookies.

index